Praise for
Red Earth

"*Red Earth*, as the title as vividly suggests, is rooted in the body of the world we inhabit, and is underpinned by an ecopoetics that grounds the human in the earthy. It is beautifully attentive to the breath and movement of the human body across different landscapes, alive to the intimations of each special place, and alert to the promptings of experience and memory. It is an assured, mature debut, real poems that renew your faith in the lyric, in the embrace of the human and the natural."

— Boey Kim Cheng, author of *Somewhere-bound, Another Place* and *Days of No Name*

"*Red Earth* lures readers into lyrical and hypnotic dream landscapes, then transports us to the quiet yet grounded textures of her tender relationships with loved ones. The earth and ocean, nonhuman creatures, stones and fossils are alive and dynamic forces in her inner psyche. Land, inheritance, migration are themes engaged through an intimate yet questing voice. The soft and precious are witnessed alongside the horrific and profane, with the unwavering gaze of a pilgrim who asks us not only to imagine what had been; but also, what could be possible."

— Lydia Kwa, author of *Oracle Bone* and *The Walking Boy*

"*Red Earth* is a miracle mirror house of contrasts, one that only superb writing can build. Using the common genre of the coming of age story, Esther has written a book as idiomatic and fluid as a sea wave. Touching on the themes of nature, she has created work that possesses some of the most sophisticated ecological poetics I have ever read. Using the wide syntactic fields of blank verse, she has shaped a concise, unique, organic style. She draws on her history and the complex history of her present, finding complex narrative about capitalism, feminism, and her own personal cultural history in her turbulent vision of nature. She creates tremendous power from a style that avoids the grand poetic gesture, has roots in the masters of her free form, and is burgeoned by a gift of metaphor that does more in a few stanzas than a book's worth of rhetoric. *Red Earth* is a book that makes the world big and small in all the sublime ways."

— Robert Lashley, author of *Green River Valley*

"Esther Vincent Xueming is a poet who feels a deep kinship and compassion with all sentient beings and the 'red earth, vast and unknowable.' Through this book, she invites us on a pilgrimage across the diverse ecologies of islands and cities, family trees and migrations, memories and dreams, language and silence. Ultimately, these poems teach us how to listen humbly to the undercurrents of every 'delicate moment'."

— Craig Santos Perez, co-founder of Ala Press and author of *From Unincorporated Territory [guma']*

"*Red Earth* is a monsoon that lingers on the evening air and sinks deep into the mother soil."

— Conner Bouchard-Roberts, publisher of Winter texts and author of *Pocket Guide to Wandering*

"'How do you reclaim a capsized past?' In *Red Earth*, Esther Vincent Xueming embarks on a journey through dreams, myths, fragments of family history and far-flung wanderings in search of ways to anchor 'the tap root of my being.' Her poems are a layered discovery of connections beyond family. Migratory birds following ancient flyways must adapt to disrupted habitat to survive. Similarly, our own disrupted lives will be rooted and nourished when we relearn to attend to what the natural world offers."

— Gina Hietpas, author of *Terrain*

"Esther Vincent Xueming's *Red Earth* is a visceral communication with the universe. Her poems are healing odes to our trembling environment. They stem from a great reverence for everything that inhabits the planet — living or non-living — rock, stone, root, sap or the flesh and psyche of human beings. She is emotionally sutured to the preservation of the intrinsic energy of life: 'With each breath, I reverse/every tectonic tremor, reshaping/land, returning to the beginning'. Even her dreams are invested in restoring a sense of balance to all that has suffered the consequences of an excessive, exploitative lifestyle. Her verses resonate with a powerful ecofeminist sincerity to combat the onslaught of modern and postmodern industrialisation. Esther is an awakened soul and her work reflects immense dignity, justice and 'love [for]/the taste/of careless freedom/the sweet hollow/of buoyant ribs that carry/us/along/unchartered coasts/our endless home'. This book is for those who want to fight for the very breath they inhale and for those who revere the primordial urge to keep sacrosanct our earth and its ecology."

— Vinita Agrawal, author of *Two Full Moons*
and editor of *Open Your Eyes*

"Esther Vincent Xueming is a seeker, both epistemologically and emotionally. In her oceanic imagination, she dives, zooms in, swoops, turns over stones. One can't help but be swept along by her peripatetic hunger through space and time, as if discovering Earth for the very first time: fresh, unencumbered, porous. Her sensual verse encompasses multitudes, from Inuit and Hindu mythologies to island sojourns to astronomy and finally, to unknowable depths of familial topography. From awe to experience, the best poems here thrive in their tactile relish of intertextuality and nature — the 'brush of grey cloud' under the 'Egg Moon', or the tattoo artist's 'hum/and whirr of metal on wet flesh'. Evolving, becoming, filled 'with patchwork and guessing', her palpable longing (for communion, for clarity) seeps from these pages into the tap root of every reader."

— Yeow Kai Chai, author of *One to the Dark Tower Comes*

"I am struck by how deftly Esther weaves together ideas about memory, dreamscapes, family history, travel and the natural environment. Her voice is clear though never didactic and her vision unwaveringly sharp as she urges the reader to gaze with new lenses at this one earth we inhabit alongside other creatures we have destroyed or ignored for too long in the anthropocene. With sensitivity and grace, Esther distils a range of emotions from experiences and encounters with significant others and with nature that vibrate and resonate powerfully with the reader. The earth emerges in all its raw beauty and fragile glory from her poetry. *Red Earth* is an excellent debut from an up-and-coming poet."

— Angelia Poon, author of *Enacting Englishness in the Victorian Period: Colonialism and the Politics of Performance*

"These poems blur, distance, vibrate, drift, refuse to come into focus, because in the phantasmagoria of the world they find wonder and consolation. Their spiritual companions are bold silhouettes, mythical creatures, and imaginary friends, not just the recurring butterflies, moths, and birds, but also the poet's dog, Ealga, who is seen as 'a kite in the wind' lovingly and surprisingly."

— Jee Leong Koh, author of *Snow at 5 PM: Translations of an insignificant Japanese poet*

"*Red Earth* is a highly distinctive achievement, a debut collection of poetry that attests to Esther Vincent's keen intelligence, painstaking craft, and searching imagination. The subjects of the poems are on one level personal, revisiting as they do family stories, memories, observations of the natural world, the privacy of dreams, and her work as a poet. In their movement, however, they surprise constantly with their reach and scope, so that to visit an out-of-the-way tourist site in Singapore or a small neighbouring island is to come unexpectedly into touch with ancient landscapes and deep layers of time, to reflect upon her forebears is to be drawn into lost and recovered histories of migration, and to note in passing tiger moths on a twig, finger, and wall is to apprehend for a rare instant the extraordinary coincidence of 'wings that beat time/to a child's ragged breath'. Invigorating Vincent's poetry contrapuntally is an avid attempt to take hold of the earth she inhabits (trees and their roots are recurring motifs) and, at the same time, a quiet yearning (in images of dreams and the sea) for what lies beyond her grasp, even the need itself 'to forget my need/for words and language' – a poetics in other words that holds promise for other interesting work to follow."

— Shirley Chew, editor of *Moving Worlds: A Journal of Transcultural Writings*

Red Earth

Poems by
Esther Vincent Xueming

Indigenous is a birthright word.
No amount of time or caring changes history
or substitutes for soul-deep fusion
with the land.

— Robin Wall Kimmerer

Many have stamped themselves
with the ink of exile.
But you, my daughter
from a land of many waters—
belong to the world.

— Grace Nichols

Nevertheless, become an oasis for all things.

— Hafiz

Contents

Dream fruit

Dream fruit 14
A different time 15
Brianna 17
In this dream, we drove into the sea 18
Island city 19
We have forgotten 20
Involuntary travel 22
Whale dream 23
The art of meditation: In four parts 24
Nocturne 27
Crossing 28
Red earth: Two variations 30
Little Guilin 33
Lavender 36

About love

About love, or a beautiful tree 40
Walk 42
Flvctvat nec mergitvr 43
My father's hands 44
Family tree 47
Lost tongue 49
In this photograph 51
Inheritance 54
The Blue Mountains 56
Throw me in the landfill 58
Sungei Buloh sonnets 60
Nondescript 62
Albatross 63
State land 64
Falcon 67

Pilgrims

Le Morne beach 70
Pilgrims 71
Solar eclipse 72
Spinning 73
Everything is perfect from far away 76
We wanted to hold on to the feeling 79
Montenegro in two scenes 81
Monsoon 83
Yogyakarta triptych 85
And at once I knew, I was not magnificent 88
Memory stone: In fragments 90

Acknowledgements 95
About the Author 97

Dream fruit

Dream fruit

I have seen the tree of my dreams,
branches dripping with the weight
of ripe fruit, shiny and inedible. In dreams,
nothing is as it seems. A tree is still a tree
even if its fruits are stones of the semi-precious kind.
In dreams, good and evil exist. I tend to have little control
over anything. Sometimes, this lack of agency
is deadly. I must have wandered off from my tree
when the noiseless phantom looters came.
But I could not see them so I could not stop
it from happening. Too late, and though
she never blamed me, I wake up always guilty.
The pain of unspeakable loss:
my inconsolable grief, that striking heap.

A different time

After William Matthews' "A Happy Childhood"

A field of grass. Common weeds of sunflower stock:
kanching baju's furry, golden head, common vernonia's soft
white breath and Cupid's shaving brush in bloom. I clutch

these wildflowers in my fist, a gift for my mother
who watches from the kitchen, as she peels the papery skin
of an onion, chopping it into deft cubes.

Tiger moths on a twig, on my finger,
on corridor walls. Wings that beat time
to a child's ragged breath. The thrill

of bathing, the tangle of arms and legs in water.
My sisters and I tunnel through cupboards for hidden
treasure, knuckles pinking from knocking on solid walls.

A sand-filled playground reeks
with the memory of overnight piss.
Leaky condoms under a swing. I watch

wrestling on the TV one day.
At night, a pale, swollen face enters my dreams.
I hold my father's hand all night to forget

this nightmare. My mother hurls a porcelain cat
at my father. He grabs her slender wrists,
bruises accidental blossoms on her skin.

My sisters orbit unscathed,
jumping on my heaving sternum.
The tiger moths disappear for a time.

Hopping on the drains one day, I miss
a step, fall. As the wound heals,
the scab peels back into a keloid ridge,

the body's way of remembering.
My mother hands me a bottle of soap,
her ballooning cheeks sighing

into the plastic wand.
The heady, synthetic smell of gum
in tiny tubes. I squeeze a dollop,

spin it with a straw, puff.
Watch it stretch, tremble
in the sun.

Another birthday celebration.
Friends who freeze into old photographs,
tucked in the bottom drawer.

Before I turn thirteen, we will sell this flat, move out,
shut the gates to a place that will return
only in my sleep. Another family now breathes

in those rooms. The field overgrown
by another high-rise. Sometimes, the past is better left
to be unearthed in dreams, where I cross

familiar streets, turn each memorised corner,
walk the same red road tiles back home
to a different time, wildflowers still wet in my grip.

Brianna

Dream sister. You vanished one night
and I know they did it
because then they tried to take me too.
Bound supine, my hair started to blaze
with the patient heat of fire, the fear
of burning alive. That morning, a butterfly
flew past my window. What little wings, strong
ascension into the shelterless wind.
Symbol of the soul, of resurrection, of hope
and life, butterfly of my waking moments, sister
of my sleep. Were they afraid
of your resistance, no longer content
to submit? Forgive me sister. I fed you the embers
of dissent, stirring something within.

In this dream, we drove into the sea

I knew it was a dream, because for one, you were driving
without a license, and two, I was comfortable enough to let you.
I told you how nice it was that you were at the wheel,
and I could just sit back. For some reason, we both knew
we had to go into the water. The back window was down,
and the car was starting to fill. Ealga was with us, our dog.
The car kept moving forward underwater, but also downward.
To be submerged and entrapped. *Let's get out of here*, I said,
sensing a portal above which would take us home.
You see, we'd been trying to return with Ealga the entire time.
We tried a bus before this but had no luck. So now, the car.
Swimming in the water, towards the sun. Holding our breaths
before bursting for air. Yes, there was an opening. Relief
that this time, we wouldn't drown. Home still distances away.

Island city

something is   happening   to my   city
this body   is leaking   rain   it goes on
for days   like the pounding   of angry fists or
drums of   war   I watched a   video of cars
trapped by water along   an industrial   street
and recalled   my dream   driving into the   sea
it beckoned   a siren singing   invisible and deep
but I could not   stop I could not   stop   myself
from sinking   the   taste of rain   yesterday
made me want   to weep   another video   of green
trash bins   white   wooden paddle boats   and
voices   over the recording   howling   shrieking
at the beach   screams   into the   unknown void
blown   by a force impossible to   measure
with an anemometer   we don't get   winds
like these   here in this   city of steel   towers rising
we don't get rain   like these   here on this   island
how do you   sleep when   your body your   city is
drowning   how do you   reclaim   a capsized past

We have forgotten

A response to Dapunta Hyang: Transmission of Knowledge by Zai Kuning

                how to love   the taste   of careless freedom
the sweet hollow   of buoyant ribs   that carry   us
    along   unchartered coasts   our endless home
                                there was a time
      when
                    people had gills   instead
of lungs   & breathing   did not matter
                              there was a   time
     when   we would scrape   the   scales   off
            each other's   limbs   every February
   in time
       for the monsoon   to wash   us dry
                     do you
                             remember
the boats   we carved from
                    the husk   of our sun-dried   bodies?
  gnarled fingers   fastened   each   bone
                        upon weathered bone
         with crimson wax   binding all futures
    to every known past
                 it is said   that once you   drink
   from   briny lips   you must never
                        look back
        there are columns   of salt

beached on   the shore
                            to prove it   I was told
                                    that once the   plaintive shoreline
turns into a bed of green moss   it is time
                                            for us to exchange   the ropes of
   our freedom   for the anchor   of dry land
I remember   waking up   one night   to find   broken
                                                                                        fingers
                                    sewn to my hands   & I had forgotten
        how to serenade   my lonesome lover   the sea
                                                    I could   not
                            tell   the names
        of each offshore island or the faces
                                                            of   each stone
my gills had left   me   breathless   & there   I stood
                                                            naked   & rooted
                        to a guilty coast

Involuntary travel

See the Egg Moon's soft yellow glow,
that brush of grey cloud just hanging beneath,
against the midnight sky? The binoculars bring her closer
and her craters resemble the cracks
on the luminescent sphere in my palm, the stone
named after the moon. As I try to sleep afterwards, a void opens
and I am an involuntary traveller, curious and awake
on an unknown path. No shape, no form, no body,
just consciousness drifting in a black, bottomless
cave of being. No sight, smell or taste,
just soft voices conversing in echoes and hums
of another tongue. A dipping in and out of time.
Two open doors. The fear of being swallowed alive
if I let myself unfold into the night.

Whale dream

I enter the sea in my dream and a great humpback
swims in the deep. Legend tells of a giant
whose fingers were cut by her father Anguta.
Sinking into the sea, they took whale form.
Are you the goddess Sedna, Mother
of the Deep? Whale of my dreams,
I have seen you glued together by plastic trash
outside a museum. I have heard your song
under a full moon calling me. A heartbeat,
drumming into my bones, then the deep tenor
of your underwater refrain echoing
into the chamber of my soul. Great mother,
I dive into the depths of your being.
Will you come speak with me?

The art of meditation: In four parts

1   *The breath*

If there is one, I have yet to learn it. What I know
is the inconstancy of sensations. Sitting in the park, cross-legged
on a wooden bench, eyes closed, heart slowing down
from the sprint, ears reaching out to the buzz of traffic,
then tuning in to the nearby tree, where the oriole whistles
her deep-throated refrain, singing herself into the morning.
She is not alone. The wind is here too, and I feel
her breath on the hairs of my neck and arms.
A gathering of tremors from deep within, so faint
at first, erupts from the base of my spine, encircling
my body. Then, a loud hush. Through layers of rock and earth,
gravel and concrete, underground trains wheeze
their mechanical coming and going. I smile, holding
this tremulous secret in the still lake of my body.

2   *Aura*

Still, the body finds a way to inhabit time.
The mind has a habit of wandering
to random thoughts, taking conscious effort to return
to the breath. Expand and collapse. The breath's journey
is cyclical, like Inanna's descent to the Underworld
where she dies and is reborn. Air fills you, leaves you,
and is changed by you. Thoughts do not matter; the body

was created to ensure its own survival.
This time, a tingling in my fingertips, and I sense
a storm brewing between my palms, augmenting
and diminishing with their shifting distance.
Turning my gaze from my hands to their shadow,
I search for colour and meaning against a white wall.
The blur of soft whiteness, the dispersion of fire blue light.

3   *Purple gate*

Beyond the woods of the mind there is a gate
and beyond that, a clearing. Not many find
this gate, some never know it exists.
The trees do a good job of hiding it.
Once, I lay down with my eyes closed and walked
out of my body, through the purple gate
and into a field of silence.
Everything seemed to vibrate
with meaning. I grew wings, becoming a moth
suspended in time, flitting in the dazzling sunlight.
I was a bat in an unlit cave, descending
into the rabbit hole of my mind.
Falling deeper into an empty well, then hauled
back into the armour of my body.

4   *Awakening the serpent*

The Hindus believe we are born
with a sacred gift coiled at the base of our spine,
the feminine divine, a sleeping serpent waiting
to be awakened. I begin my practice by shaking
my pelvis, letting go of my ego, feeling my skin moult.
A fire. It shoots to my crown, and I surrender
to its hot charge and release. Is this what it feels like
to lose control? To imbibe the universe, to free
the self from the heaviness of the body?
Ong namo guru dev namo.
A new sensation, of lightning and ice rising
within me, breaking wave upon wave of sweetness
and light, burning. A slow uncoiling, a tentative
hiss, a lustrous slithering from root to crown.

Nocturne

Again, the night. Again, the sleep
that does not come.
I grow tired of this cloud gathering
into an alert restlessness beside you.
In the living room, I turn on the lights,
try to read to forget my need
for sleep. I sit at the table and write a poem
about the night, sleep and song.
Chopin's nocturne.
I used to sit for hours at my piano, clumsy fingers
committing each note to memory.
But genius cannot be imitated, nor darkness
summoned at will.
I find I have drifted, so I return
to this room. A light wind wafts
in, blessing me with its touch. The lure
of open windows at night, the promise
of cricket songs and frogs after the rain.
The air hangs heavy outside this frame
and nothing is clear
in this light, where even resident trees
are made strange
by the park lamp's flicker
and my poor vision at night.
The only frogs I see in the day lie
with their bellies on top. They live
for the night, I think, for the moon's half
gaze, the silent gush of velvety wings
across a charcoal sky.

Crossing

A tribute, after William E. Stafford's "Travelling through the Dark"

The sambar deer in the photograph is folded
onto the street, red cloth over her eyes,
a bead of sweat hanging
from her lips. I see through my screen

how she is still alive, brown torso upright
after the hit, but by the time I read this news
her body is cold, she is no longer breathing,
put to death by a team of experts. A luckless way to go.

The article says she was in great distress.
I imagine the screech and crash, the great impact,
honkings and bright headlights, legs weak
and impotent. The stress of sitting still, waiting

for a dignified end. And though I never
knew her, I want to remember.

*

Imaginary friend, let me resurrect
your broken body from the dirt and ash.
Let your soul re-enter the world of the living
through this breath, as you rise again

to reclaim the earth with your quiet existence.
Perhaps you will choose to walk calmly
along a secluded road, or chew on grass
in a clearing, your head bowed low, eyelids soft

and content. Why do you share this forest, knowing
we will betray you one day? You do not speak, but look
at me gently, holding my gaze in a deep pool
of endless knowing. You teach me to forget my need

for words and language. You teach me to stay
in this delicate moment: in our eyes, our reflections crossing.

Red earth: Two variations

Awake
After a Raden Saleh painting of Java

Broken earth, you are a strange specimen,
unearthing along the streets of Batam like a cinnabar wave,
conjuring an old Javanese landscape

against the setting sun. Fading amber rays
of an apricot sky. A chain of ageless mountains.
Fine details smudge into soft lines, unfolding distances,

unrolling time. Finger, oil and canvas unveil
a forgotten world. Later that evening, I will drowse
by the pool, drawn towards the same orange sun

in his undressing. The silhouette of trees keeps a watchful eye
on transient visitors like me, our coming and going
constant as the pull of the moon on the sea.

This image is less poetic, and I am no artist, so I use words
to paint a scene of red earth, vast and unknowable.

Asleep

Red earth, you are a strange specimen.
Unearthing along the streets of Batam,

I cannot tell what minerals compose you,
or why your redness excites me.

You are known by many names.
Red bauxite ore.
Child of the Riau.
Blood. Bread.
Sedimentary rock.
Soil of the people.
Mother of the land.

But you are just the earth, red
earth, to me.

*

Once, I dreamt I was bathing in red earth,
sighing as I pushed my fingers deep
into the night of her abdomen, to uncover
the lost roots of felled trees.
To mine the subconscious. To enter the darkness.
The earth as a metaphor for my body,
vast and unknowable.

*

What I know asleep, how can I utter awake?

The earth grows redder
no matter what I feed her.

*

Wrap me in your thickening fog.
Let me crawl back into your hollow womb,
steeped in endless sleep.

Little Guilin

Skyscrapers tower behind you
as you sleep. You were here
in the beginning.

Before asphalt swallowed the ground
beneath you, before each brick
was laid, layer

upon layer rising above you.
Before you were given your name,
you were here.

But I have only now discovered you.
Let me begin then, at the beginning.

Walking from Bukit Batok Central,
forest foliage bordering the roadside,
we meandered through a park on a hill,

lured by bird song, cicadas
and rhythmic chants from a nearby temple.
We found you beyond the road's left spine,

a granite lotus hovering above water.
Time has turned you from stone
into myth; your weather-chiselled face—

rock grey, orange, chalk white,
is all that remains
of the millions of nights you have spent

under the moon's watchful light. A silence seeps
into my being, and I sense a quivering
hanging in the air.

Eyes closed, I trace in each gradient
of rock a forgotten layer in time.
With each breath, I reverse

every tectonic tremor, reshaping
land, returning to the beginning.

In the beginning, ancient norite collapses
into granite, sinking into the softness
of the earth's sternum.

Viscous and smouldering,
molten rock returns
to the ovum of unborn volcanoes.

Primordial mantle of fire and ice,
your lungs churn darkness and light.

In the beginning, there is a sound
the earth makes when her eyelids twitch
after a long slumber.

It is a rolling thunder I cannot hear,
a call so old I cannot enter.

Lavender

After "Tha Mo Ghaol Air Aird A'Chuain"

Months after the wedding, the musk
of lavender still retains

its potency, soaking the living room air.
The bouquet is dried by the sun

and the ceiling fan's breathy swirls,
initiating each bud into the afterlife.

Was it only last evening that I held your hand
in mine, sharing a glass of Kilbeggan

as we made our way towards the ivy arch?
Our hands winding that blue and golden cord

light and fast around our wrists, the weight
and measure of our love bound

into a single knot.
The faint scent of lavender whorling

through time into memory.
Now, you sleep to the song

of a woman from another time, singing
for her husband to return from sea,

in a language we can and cannot understand.
It is a song of longing, of a blue autumn

without her boatman, her rare and steadfast love
a bouquet of lavender, blue thistle

and soft green cinerea, beginning
as song, lingering as scent.

About love

About love, or a beautiful tree

After Eavan Boland's "Quarantine"

You write about love in a time of darkness,
a time of Great Hunger,

of a man who loved his wife more than his life,
he carried the weight of his love

and walked for miles north
into the cold, starry night,

her feet held against his breastbone.
The last heat of his flesh his last gift to her.

Teach me to write a poem about love.
One in which I carry the weight

of my love upon my shoulders,
scarred feet tucked into my breastbone,

as I walk into the freezing dark.
Teach me to be like the man in the poem,

giver of last heat.
Teach me to be you.

In this poem, we head north.
We walk until we find a place

to rest and bury our bodies, two trees
returning to the earth as flesh.

Roots growing into each other, twinning
underground. Fed by the elements above,

our branches seeking to inosculate self
into other with the patience of time.

Years pass and we forget
a time before rootedness, before love.

In time, wood too turns to stone,
and as our bones mineralise and petrify,

the weight of our love will crystallise
into fossil, grounding the heart.

Walk

For Ealga

The dog sits before me with a serious look, reminding me
there is a walk to be made, a circuit of streets, construction sites,
school zones, park connectors to be traversed, fresh and new

each day. She breaks into a trot, tongue out, eyes bright,
legs scissoring across concrete, leading me by that cord
binding my wrist to her neck. Like a kite in the wind, she drifts

away, closes in, moving by instinct and the curiosity of scent.
We navigate shifting distances, our bodies sharing one rhythm.
Wide cracks furrow the thirsty ground. Grasses browned

by the heat. We are alone in the field again, now a partial work site.
She strains eastwards, towards the cordoned-off canal, where she senses
an opening. I am learning to trust her, to lower my body down to the earth,

step into the canal's mouth, to occupy the space between control
and release. She waits, patient and still, fully present in this moment.
Her hazel eyes are freckled and deep with knowing, soft

as they tell me this truth: Take your time, ready yourself. I am here
to guide you. She looks over and I signal back. Back arched,
muscles taut, she pulls and springs across the chasm, her body
a noiseless white arrow, black diamond on her head.

Flvctvat nec mergitvr

I surrender my body to an ancient art, skilled hands marking
and wounding, needles entering layers of the psyche, transforming pain

into healing. The tattoo artist's hands rest on my right thigh as he bends
and labours over his art, my body, bringing me towards my becoming.

First, he shaves my skin, then carefully transfers the template,
tracing the black outline. For six long hours, the intermittent hum

and whirr of metal on wet flesh, lemon cake and toilet breaks.
Shading for depth and colour, which shocks and sears

my back, nerves writhing and pulling with each precise dip.
One learns to stay calm and breathe. One learns to ride the storm.

The body as a map to be written and read, navigating the shifting tides.
This is the path I have chosen, to chart a course into the open

with a purple compass, sea green anchor, frayed rope and the blessings
of two sea birds, wings outstretched, circling.

My father's hands

For my father

My father's hands are dark
from prolonged exposure to the sun.
With those hands, he fixes

air compressors forgotten at the back
of sweating factories.
His palms are red. I remember

wishing mine were red like his.
How we used to press
our palms together, to measure

how fast I was growing.
My father's hands guide me from pillar
to pillar as I roll on wheels, reaching

for the great beyond.
At twelve, he tattoos an anchor
in blue ink into the curve

between his thumb and forefinger.
He talks about removing it, and I touch
my right thigh, tracing seafoam green,

anchors searching for dry land.
Moored yet adrift
in the sea of our being.

*

In a lost jotter book,
my father pencils miniature animals
in lead: deer, bird, dog, cat.

He takes my hands and we roll over
the snare and tom-toms
in church, my father making it look

so easy.
Many childhoods ago,
my father caught spiders with his hands,

climbed over fences
and into drains to catch fish.
In an old photograph,

he carries me with two hands,
a young and handsome father beaming
into the future.

*

He keeps his tattoo.
He continues to work
with his hands, just as he loves

with his hands, ironing my dress,
clipping my nails, cutting an apple.
When I move out and my cupboard breaks,

he comes down with a spare hinge.
The dog is curious. He pats her soft head
with his right hand, the same hand

that held me to sleep during a nightmare.
My electric switch is faulty.
I text him, and he arrives with a new box.

Pass me the Phillips head?
I tilt my flashlight into the darkness
as he shows me how to connect

live to live,
neutral to neutral,
earth to earth.

Family tree

1

A past that remains out of my reach. Fractured
crown, my family tree leaves me wondering
about its gaping silences. My father's memory
only travels two generations in time to arrive

at an origin. James Nanayakkara from Ceylon
and his Tamil wife. My father recalls an anecdote:
his grandmother and father sprawled on the living room floor,
buzzing from cheap liquor on hot afternoons.

My father's mother, whose ancestry stops
at the "Gate of Hope", orphaned as an infant.
Raised by French nuns, she was christened Nelly.
Who was her mother? Why did she leave? The history

of my becoming in fragments. Three countries
and an ocean, harbouring lost stories of migration.

2

Forefathers and nameless women
who crossed the seas to build new homes
on foreign land. Elopements,
estrangements, women leading hard lives

as orphans, single mothers, second wives.
Men who changed their names to suit the climate
of the times. Lives that blur and coalesce
from the forgetfulness of bitter years, lines

reaching out across the white expanse
of time and space, in search of a history.
An exile to my past, I fill this void
with patchwork and guessing, my longing

bleeding from the margins of the page
into the tap root of my being.

Lost tongue

After Sujata Bhatt's "Search for my tongue"

Just as Sujata Bhatt searched
for her tongue
to find that she had not one
but two, the native more foreign
than the other, I too long to fill my mouth
with the lost vowels and sacred
consonants of my mother tongue.

                                                Mama mokakda?

How do I translate
my desire to connect
with a language inherited in my veins,
one that never found its sounds?
How can I make sense of strange
graphemes that curlicue meaning
out of curious lines?

                                        Memagin kumak veyida?

Today I learnt the merit of speaking
in idioms, for instance,
කණ කොකාගෙ සුදු පෙනෙන්නේ ඉගිලුනාමලු
kana kokaage suda penenne igilunaamalu
(the whiteness of a crane appears only when it flies)
which is to say, a thing's beauty emerges
only upon its leaving.

There must be a way

to accurately transliterate my sorrow

into the sound of regret. But after two tries

Google turns "sorrow" into "sorry" as in

> I am sorry I do not know how to say this.

> I am sorry I lost my tongue.

> I am sorry I saw the crane only in time for it to take flight.

In this photograph

For my mother

1

It is 1982. She is twenty-one.
It is her birthday and she is in full bloom, generous
to friends who have come like bees, drawn
to the nectar of her youth, radiating

off the twirls of her skirt as she spins. I wonder
which song was playing over the stereo, what beats
she moved to, her limbs swaying to the rhythm
of carefree abandon, eyes half-closed.

Her red lips, smiling. She is a moving image
in white, her dress giddy at the folds
of her pleated skirt, her straight jet black hair cut
at the fringes into uniform bangs.

Dancing, drinking, she savours
each last fading beat.

2

Twelve years will pass.
She is now a mother of two.
A younger version of myself
clutches her right leg, my sister her left.

She is well settled into the role of mother,
pale, resolute, unrelenting.
We trust her with every decision,
from dressing us

in matching rainbow-coloured tights
or identical white flare dresses
to our bowl-cut fringes
that turn us into miniatures of her.

We sit on her lap, mute
and malleable as wet clay.

3

She is a moving image, changing,
        shape-shifting with the seasons
but still the same.

        I hear her voice and imagine
how she would have led that kampung life, a child
        throwing that bucket deep into the family well, the crash

of cold water. Then the slow haul up, bucket resting
        on stone, the tremble of its full liquid weight
up the hill on that small frame.

        Her mother working from door to door
washing the undergarments of strangers
        till the water left her palms dry with cracking.

4

Mother, you are golden now
though your hairs have turned grey.

Your body spins slowly, and your spirit
is hard and soft at the same time.

Your voice no longer rings shrill
but when I talk you listen,

in this photograph that never yellows
with age or fades into memory.

You are an image both clear
and out of focus,

shifting yet still, brimming
with the blur of whiteness spinning.

Inheritance

At thirty-two, I am beginning to learn
that my story is not my own,
my body a birthing of inherited sorrow.

Pointing at a woman in a faded photograph,
my mother tells me great-grandmother was a cripple.
I see the wooden stump peeking out

from light blue cotton pants, where warm flesh
should be. I ask my grandmother about her.
Grandmother speaks in the lilting tones of Cantonese,

slurring her vowels. My mother mediates
our broken speech, something about stepping
on a rusty nail, the rot and swell of gangrene.

Great-grandmother's body maps a loss
my grandmother now inherits, both legs tethered
to a wheelchair. Once, during the Occupation,

grandmother's legs carried her across the Causeway,
her little brother on her back. She was only seven.
Those legs would never return

to her childhood home, but take root
here, as she walked from door to door in search of work
that would leave my mother at home, alone.

Now, my mother sits with her legs stretched out
beside mine. Spider veins like purple tributaries web
her calves. Skin like parchment from neglect.

Her left foot rocking to the steady tap
and hum of her vintage Singer, pedalling
her love into the seams of my dress.

Beside her, my feet are overgrown, marked
by rivulets of green. My right foot learnt to move
to a different kind of rhythm, my heel a pivot.

The step and release on the faded brass pedals
of my second-hand K. Kawai,
my feet a muddy echo of my mothers.

Fingers trilling black and white, I turn
the page, keep time with the metronome's steady
beat, tapping live, live, live.

The Blue Mountains

Twenty-one years ago, my parents sold
our four-room apartment so we could travel

south. I remember Sydney, the Opera House,
the Blue Mountains. Dogs furry and big

as grown sheep. The clear mist of mountain air,
the plunging cable ride to the Three Sisters, their stony,

ancient forms standing still and foreboding
in the quiet valley. I told my mother I would retire

there one day. Twenty years later, bushfires would sweep
across the mountains, not discriminating between bird

or tree, insatiable in its taking. Everywhere, fire
and smoke thickening, darkening the sky.

Millions die, their charred bodies lying side
by side on a scorched black earth while I sit unscathed

in front of a screen trying to process my grief.
Of all the photographs, this: a joey hugging

a wire fence, its charcoal face smiling at the camera,
its young leathery body now dusty and crumbling.

What bravery, what foolhardiness, what bliss,
to give death one final grin before the fire came for him too?

Australia is burning, and the mountains of my memory
are turning blue. I think how this poem

could be a leaking hose running out of water
to quench a dry and angry land. But I also think

how it could be brimming, undefeated, full
of life in its last breath before the raging dark.

Throw me in the landfill

For Pulau Semakau and Pulau Sakeng

Standing near the breakwater, looking out for miles,
no other land. The air cradles the briny perfume
of the sea, carrying memories of laughing children running
barefoot on makeshift boardwalks, diving like thirsty fish

into water, a kampung life long washed away from the shore.
Restless waves beat time against the rocks, waiting.
In time, the fire turns all things to ash in this landfill
whose blue lungs are fading grey.

To trade water for solid ground, a kingdom for a grain
of sand. Stolen memories of home, of a people forced
to give up their gills for breathing in exchange
for webbed feet that drag across dry land.

A city might forget, but the land,
she finds a way to remember.

*

Pulau Semakau, Pulau Sakeng,
now debris-choked
and dusty, pillaged
into a nondescript wasteland.

In time, your bunds will break,
the waters will rise
and you will launch your boats
back to sea.

But you already know this,
so you sleep for now, patient,
as a Brahminy kite circles out of your dreams,
sweeping over the sky

into my limited vision,
crying out a solitary *keeyew*.

Sungei Buloh sonnets

1 *Migratory birds*

A long drive in. Binoculars to help with seeing.
We are here for migratory birds flying in
from as far as Alaska, Siberia, Far East Russia,
arriving by ancient flyways like those that have come before.
They will stop, eat, gather their strength on this mudflat,
before some push further south. Born with migration
mapped into their genes, they listen to instinct,
departing for warmer climes, returning home in spring.
I turn the knob. A sandpiper perching on a river log,
happy in its solitude. At the lookout, whimbrels,
red and green shanks, stand motionless, indiscernible
to the human eye. Unperturbed by these visitors,
resident hybrid storks stretch their wings in lazy aerial circles,
signalling home, even if only for a time.

2 *The mangrove*

At low tide, the prop and pencil roots of the mangrove
are visible from the ground. This is how the forest breathes,
in sync with the changing tides. The boardwalk
brings us closer, yet separates us from this briny world
where crabs climb trees every day of their lives.
As the tide rises, more seek refuge on tree trunks.
I have never been this close to crabs in the wild.
The Teochews eat them in vinegar.
A heavy rustle. The sound of wings above the trees.
We follow the movement, binoculars to eyes.
Two juvenile sea eagles back from their hunt,
rest at the edge of the wetlands, looking out to sea.
The Straits of Johor marks the boundary between here
and there. Towering columns blur the horizon.

Nondescript

After Stephen James Smith's "Nightsky & Butterfly"

It is true. I used to catch
nondescript moths in plastic
bags & wait for them to die
from concussions. Conscious.
What happens when a palm hits
a bubble? Dust. That's
what coats the tips
of my fingers when I press
them tight, sweat chaffing
at grey wings. Yesterday, a black
butterfly flew into the iris
of my periphery, and I felt a lightness
in my step. Air expands.
Yes, I used to enjoy
taunting captive moths. I'd dizzy
their capsules & watch them catapult
into stale space. I was cruel. It is not
necessary to torment the tortured.
Hindsight makes you less
guilty but you cannot escape
the fluttering. Dead wings learn
to flap long after the breath leaves
the body. I know it was wrong
to kill. Forgive me.

Albatross

On illegal sand mining in Cambodia

A country is hungry to expand her borders,
so she sucks on the fat of another's land.
Machines like ravenous knives carve out tonne
after incessant tonne of sand, dredging the body

to the marrow. Stripped bare, the mangrove's prop
and pencil roots become useless bleeding stumps.
How can she breathe air that is iron and rust?
How strange to fill the sea with sand, to reclaim

water into unsinkable land. A country builds
another tower, a floating garden of imported
flora, a casino with a capsized boat.
To carry this albatross of guilt, my shame

of standing on another's land, the weight
of a body that was never mine to own.

State land

1

The field is claimed by the sign staked
into the ground: state land.

Blue nets line the edge, turning
communal space into exile.

Will the egrets return?
Will the land forgive?

2

I remember migrant workers playing cricket
on their day off.
They would lay out rope on the field

to mark off the boundary of their makeshift pitch,
then begin to play, each time
opening up the circle

to ease each newcomer into the game.
The kite flyers, mostly elderly men, found freedom
in the skies where their feet would never tread,

bodies forever anchored to earth.
How they would captain their kites into unknown winds—
an orange stingray, a golden eagle, a red fox.

Then, there were the Frisbee players, young,
sun-kissed fools running after spinning plastic,
playing through sun or rain.

*

Now there stand, two yellow,
silent cranes, waiting.

First, they took down the rude wooden fences
one hot afternoon, erecting new posts

to partition the field
into nameless plots with blue

ghost nets.
Nets that lure and lie, that enslave

an enamoured butterfly
who thought she could reach the sky

beyond the mesh of blue.
Next came the excavator

dredging up the belly of the earth.
I recall walking past fresh wet earth, thinking

so this is what sorrow smells like,
when a mother is forced to give.

We could learn from the mynahs,
who take from her only what they need,

or the egrets, who find temporary respite,
each migration uncovering new truths, of lost

places and changed faces, of strange ghost nets
that beach themselves on state land.

3

For days the silence
haunts me,
until one evening, after the rain,
it is broken by the beating of white wings

that arrive in the distance,
encircling the lonely field.

Walking out to meet them,
I find fourteen egrets still
in the moment of the hunt,
heads bowed,

treading softly as they dip
yellow beaks into the tall, wet grass,
unperturbed by onlookers,
they and I, separated

and bound
by a gossamer blue.

Falcon

The peregrine falcon has found its way
to its roost just across my window, fifteen stories
above the ground. Perching motionless
in the afternoon sun, it stayed as the heat turned
into the shingle of rain. Perhaps it was resting,
tired out from its long journey South.
Or perhaps it was watching, patient,
waiting for the right time to dive for the kill.

Two days later, it flies to its roost with a half-eaten mynah
in its claws. This is the first time I witness a raptor eat
its prey in real-life, up close.
Binoculars to eyes, I see how it plucks
at the black feathers to get at the flesh.
I watch as they drift down to the road below,
and wonder at my own lack of sympathy.
I am rooting for the hunter, this wanderer
from the North, now feeding on the mynahs
and pigeons in our estate.
I think about bird devouring bird in a holy ritual
of predator and prey, a sacred cycle
of giving and taking.
The mynah bound to the falcon in death.
The falcon bound to the mynah for its life.
The giver releasing its spirit to another.
The taker honoring the hunt.

The falcon doesn't finish its meal,
but gathers its wings and launches off with the remains
into the evening light.

Each day, our eyes turn to the same spot,
hoping for a familiar shape. Medium-sized,
dark helmet, barred underbelly,
yellow eye-ring,
yellow hooked bill and talons.
Head-turned, the bird eyeing us in return.

Over time, we learn to decipher the clues.
Body parts of a bird, a chameleon's tail.
We read the signs like children learning the language of birds.
We admire the falcon's hard work and labour.
We yearn to inhabit its feathered body,
to ride the wind at dizzying speeds.

Earthbound, we imagine ourselves light
as paper kites each time the falcon
flies into our waking sight.
We dream ourselves winged, perching
on the tallest tree, jungle floor below.

We see with falcon eyes that we too can weather
intense heat and pouring rain.
That we can stand still
with a falcon's patience above the din of cranes,
the roar of construction.
We wear our barred plumage with the pride
of former juveniles.
We circle and drop into a well-timed death
to emerge on the other side of our dream,
shrieking with life from the tallest tree.

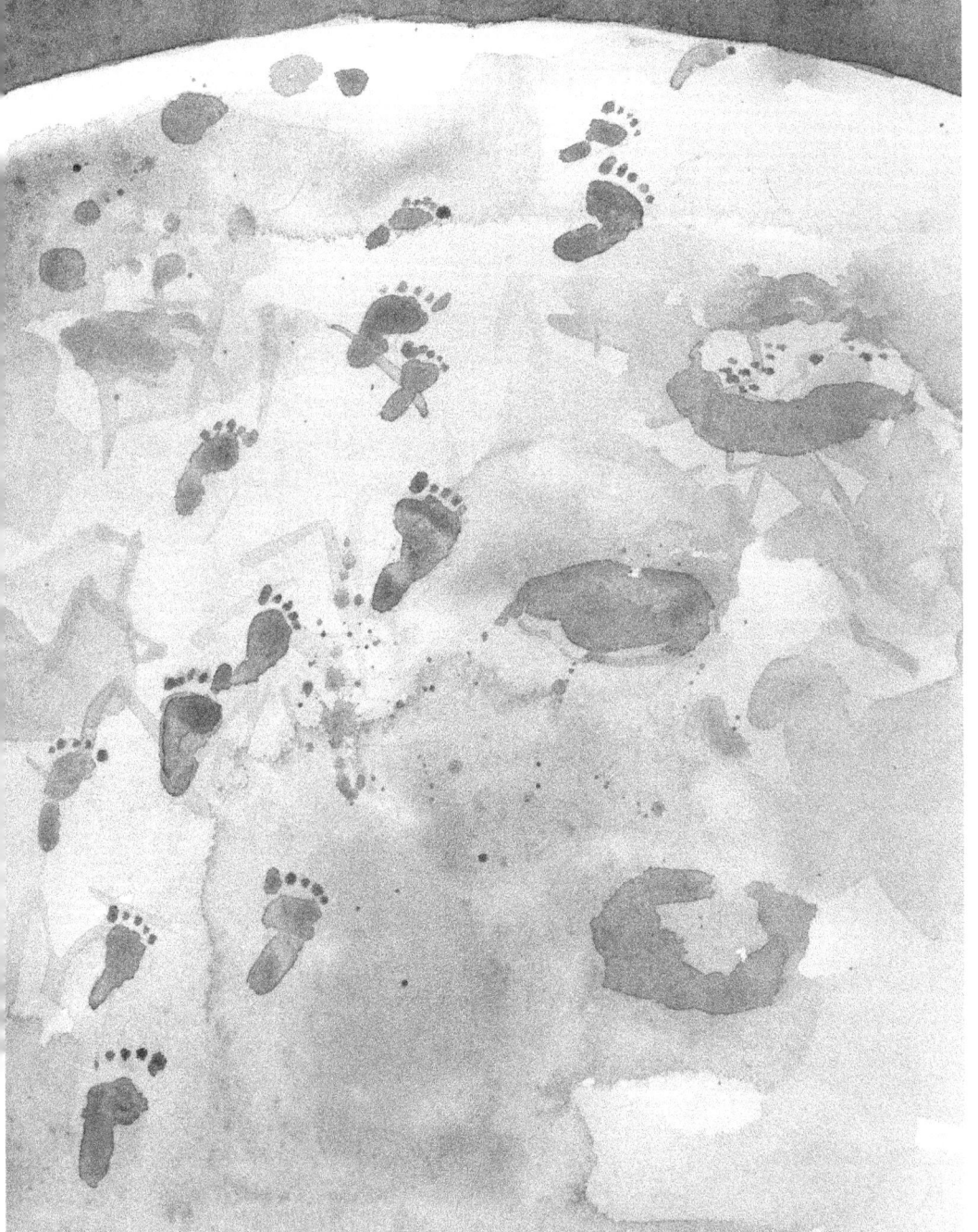

Pilgrims

Le Morne beach

After Linda Gregg's "Greece when Nobody's Looking"

The night is a new kind of blackness that surprises.
Infinite stars like crushed ice overhead. This is land birthed
by fire and water, millions of years ago. She asked,
Do you want to go and watch the sega?
Yes, he said, and they brought along the bottle.
Music on the beach, a crew directing sega dancers by bonfire
and spotlight. The sea crashing into the dazzling sky. A poetry
of blue lagoons, bleached coral and bonfires smouldering.

Pilgrims

Hiking up the Piton de la Fournaise

A bumpy ride across an ashy plateau, still misty
from the rain. The air is sulphuric, tinged with grey.
We are a motley crew of travellers, bodies shaking
in the heaving car with each cratered drop.
Ground marked by potholes reminds me of the moon.
To reach the base of the breathing volcano,
we must cross the Plaine des Sables.
The hike teaches us that the body has its limits,
that we must be patient and listen.
Carefully, we trek down the mountain's side,
on uneven steps carved out of solid rock,
an unforgiving drop to our right. Fellow hikers
daily traverse this path, treading land forged by fire, spewed
from the depths of a restless molten core, awakening
each year to remind us, it lives.
Strong, intermittent winds unsettling the dust.
As far as the eye can see, miles of dark brown rock, bulbous
and grotesque, rising towards the peak.
Rock braided into the ground like rope, gnarled
and twisted from the constant pressure of hot and cold.
I bend down to touch some porous fragments,
then wrap and keep them in my bag. Our guide
has gone on ahead, eager to make good time.
Each eruption leaves something behind, I think,
the fire giving even as it takes.
This time, we are lucky. We lose nothing but daylight.
A wandering mist swirls over the land,
taking its time to know each crevice,
name each surviving plant.
We climb the caldera, sit and eat amidst the ashes.
We shrink as the eye expands, pilgrims walking on fire.

Solar eclipse

Driving in the dark, we search for the moon
against a tall, grassy landscape. Behind,
the gaping black of a road lined with old trees.
Across the island, sugarcanes rise
and bend with the wind into the expanse
of a chalky grey sky, where the moon hangs
her round face low. The wild darkness changes
her into a strange thing, impossible
to understand. The same moon now mutely passing
between sun and earth, churning cloud and sky
into a blue phantasmagoria, turning day
to night for a time. Framed by the fronds
of tropical palms, look how the fiery sun burns,
sickle-shaped with the white brightness of his longing.

Spinning

The Ferris wheel spins,
a celestial glow-worm in the fading daylight.

Early winter in Tokyo, yet the cold cuts
four layers of fabric, chilling her bones

despite the sun. The wheel, unchanging,
draws a complete circle with each languid revolution,

marvellous machine of red and blue, defying time.
He grabs her hand and they are spindled

into the same carriage, their bodies growing lighter
with each lift, suspended in air, in time.

Down below, two rows of ducks waddle
on the grass, idly tracing their way back home

to the nearby lake, where a nonchalant black swan
stands on a rock, flapping and drying its wings.

Soon, it too becomes just another shape,
indiscernible chaos. Holding her close,

he points out landmarks, their world shrinking
to the width and height of their capsule.

See how this dome marks DisneySea,
her fictitious worlds. They could not know then

how the yellow lights of the caravan carousel
would lure them to the Arabian coast the next evening,

how they would ride around in circles
on plastic horses, giddy and young again.

As the wheel spins, they press their heads together,
shedding more of themselves—

until they are weightless and transparent,
floating in time, with only enough room

left for forgiveness.
A soundless ring

vibrates into empty space.
Time slows down into a moment

of stillness. Of a buzzing,
the confusion of distorted speech.

In that same moment, another spin,
the wheel continuing her revolution.

With each descent, the sky turns
a darker shade of orange, burning

and urgent in its setting.
Then, the cold blanket of night.

A puzzle stands on the bedroom dresser.
A photograph of the Ferris wheel

in 500 broken parts,
now form an unbroken whole.

Six winters ago, we were there—
There was a cat whisperer at the park bench,

silent in the company of three strays.
Holding on to the last breaths of light,

we ran to the observatory,
watching the sun burn itself into the sea.

An old couple on the beach,
quiet and still against a familiar sunset,

the Ferris wheel spinning
behind them.

Everything is perfect from far away

When I close my eyes,
the countryside is a happy blur
& a cool, dry breath.

A warm cup of coffee turning cold
in the subtropical morning,
the gentle Dalat winter stirring through it.

A scene comes into focus from our hotel patio—
green zinc roofs, red terracotta tiles,
the odd-coloured bungalow nestled

amidst conifers & blooming temperate greens
framed by distant hills, the countryside vanishing
into a hilltop pagoda.

Feverish from the midday heat,
we bought ourselves wings with loose change
in a pedalo on Xuan Hong lake

though our feet never left the water.
We laughed as we swatted thirsty mosquitoes,
dissolving into the lake & walking on water,

perspiring, pedalling & floating
into each other, as roadside pedlars looked on
into the honking traffic.

Do you remember the wayside flowers
painting their faces the colour of spring
all year round?

When I close my eyes,
the countryside is a happy blur
& everything is perfect from far away.

At the cable car, we re-enact a scene
from *Glück*. Bliss.
You held your scarf, flapping in the wind

as I took a snapshot. *Whoopdee.*
The whirlwind alpine coaster ride,
its thrill of speed & wind & fear.

Your arms & legs around my arms & body,
holding me in an unuttered promise
as we coasted through winding tracks

down to the heart of the waterfall.
Again, again, again.
We enter the Hang Nga Crazy House

knowing we will never return.
Le Petit Paris, when I close my eyes,
you are there in the fog

of my dreams.
An invisible door opens
& I enter its rooms on all fours.

Crouching on Elephant Falls in broken
slippers, trying hard not to slip
into the coffee cups of young lovers,

envious of how they trade eyes
with each other in one long, unbroken moment
of stillness, held together

by an endless spring
& a cup of coffee that never turns cold
in the swirling wind.

We wanted to hold on to the feeling

For Éire

of open skies and empty roads
that carry tractors into town.

Of monstrous waves crashing
against rugged white-tipped headlands

where seabirds circle and cry.
Of boarding a ferry to Inis Mor,

wind whipping our hair, piercing
through wool, as we spin through karst

country, slowing down
for curious horses, elusive seals.

We wanted to hold on to the feeling
of whispers in the wind

over fields of sleeping graves
and grazing sheep at Clonmacnoise,

of gulls above a Normandy ruin,
cawing superstitions about a river

and her name.
Of sheep bleats that echo

from hill to hill, the silence cast
by famine walls, separating

nothing, leading nowhere.
We wanted to hold on

to the feeling
of megalithic awe

at Brownshill dolmen,
of pressing our palms against cold,

ancient stone fallen in
and weathered by time.

Of running searching fingers
over each grain of barley

as we sway and dance
to the rhythm of the dolmen

in our mind's eye, evoking a song
familiar, forgotten, strange

on our tongues, the bittersweet
old religion. Of the electric

air crackling in the breeze,
so faint, almost imagined.

Montenegro in two scenes

1   *Perast*

The bus takes us into the old town.
The Bay of Kotor, where mountains
break dangerously into the sea.

We have seen her in our dreams,
and now we walk her cobbled streets, waving
at men who work to restore the old church.

Our Lady of the Rocks, flung off the coast,
she rests on the drowned bodies
of ships sunk with rocks.

To reach her, we speak with a weathered
boatman, who takes us for ten euros.
The little boat is bumpy but our boatman knows

the mood of the waves, and he rows, steady
over the choppy water.
Saline breeze, boot prints on stone.

Couples marry here today. We learn
of a tapestry, sewn by a sailor's wife
for twenty-five long years, she awaiting

his safe return, her dark hair stitched
into the votive turning grey, eye
to needle, eye to glass, her love immortalised

as the light weaved its way out of her eyes.
How she must have loved her boatman,
how tragic their lives, how lucky

we are, I think, as our little white boat tosses
on the fickle sea. The rain blesses us
in its falling, our boatman's smile

turning him into a young man
who would live to grow old one day.

2   *Cetinje*

The stray joins us mid-way on our tour, rolling over
for belly rubs, thick padded paws in the air. Digging

at earth, he sniffs, snorts, shakes his furry head while we try
to stay focused. At the monastery, he lies within the circle

of our feet, panting on his side, stretched out on stone.
Our guide returns with news that they will let us in on special terms.

The dog seems to know he has to wait, and wags his tail
when we emerge. I record him with my phone, his white tail curved high,

the sweetness of his trust, the bounce of his gait
as though he did not sleep in the cold at night, did not beg

for meals. We admire the embassies. An angry local walks by
cursing him. Goodbye is the hardest, but he teaches us

not to be sentimental. Sitting on the grass, he looks once, then turns
away as the car backs out, knowing we cannot stay.

Monsoon

The southerly winds have arrived,
and with them, occasional showers and thunderstorms
washing the afternoons down with the shingle of rain.
They will stay for four months, returning again

next June. Our plants rely on this gift of seasonal rain
to survive. We try to care for them, inventing a way
to collect the rain with a wooden pole and a small bucket,
fourteen floors above the ground. In another place,

you could walk above the water, barefoot
on wooden boards warmed by the sun. Buckets on land,
each distinctive clan making an incense offering
to the goddess Mazu, prayers coiling out to sea.

Birds on the wire signalling rain.
Fishermen's boats lie like forgotten relics berthed
along the pier, empty fish traps stacked like totems, watchful.
Plastic bottles floating in the canals, aimless and drifting.

A lone path funnels into the open straits,
where rotting wooden stumps remember old routes.
Before the storm, a grey seabird landed and folded her wings,
waiting, still. Next came the onslaught of wind and rain.

Remember how we took off our shoes, two unlikely pilgrims,
seeking shelter in the red-roofed temple,
as the rain licked away at the wood beneath our feet?
A red altar. A wrinkled orange. The temple keeper

in his shorts, his slippers, his well-poised
umbrella, lighting incense in a humble offering.
How he kept our shoes dry under a 'No Shoes' sign.
His kindness towards strangers, the lashing rain on zinc.

Yogyakarta triptych

Candi Sewu

Ruins of a temple ground,
designed to contain the cosmos.

A silence that echoes
in the sizzling heat.

I walk to feel the ground underfoot,
uncertain of what I am seeking
amidst the spiralling sand.

Dust all around. Broken universe.
I step inside the main temple and lose
      myself in its chambers,
another traveller in search of
        meaning.

Around, workers straddle the necks
      of scattered temples, chisel
      at stone,
restoring looted heads.

Prambanan

From a distance, the many faces of the
        Trimurti tower
above us, rising from myth
        into plain sight.

We scurry like ants between stone
        and shrine,
incidental devotees
        of the intermittent shade.

The sun makes his daily rounds,
        asking to enter at noon.
Every day, temple doors oblige.

We leave, learning of gods that create,
        preserve and destroy.
Like them, we too make and break
        something each day.

Candi Borobudur

Elephants on parade.
Pilgrims with umbrellas float

like lotuses
along the divine path, seeking peace.

I miss the sunrise over Borobudur
but each elevation
promises renewed light.

Buddhas in stupas, many headless.
I read in the ornate bas-reliefs, poses
      and eroded colours,
the tales of princes, thieves and
      mere commoners.

The undying rain reminds me
      of my mortality, each drop
      a chip in time.
I arrive at the top still searching.

And at once I knew, I was not magnificent

How do I write a poem about memory?

Memory as image,
an image of you, up there,
untouchable, magnificent.
You stand on Arthur's Seat,
camera strap slung around your neck
like a noose threatening
to tighten, asphyxiate if not careful.

The image begins
with stepping through park gates, leaving
the city behind us to grow smaller
and smaller still
as we trek dirt roads uphill
and walk through green fields
to reach the mountain.

You capture each fragile moment—
scattered fort ruins,
yellow gorse dotting the hills, a remnant
of the Scottish spring,
the quiet valley below, a miniature city
far out of reach.

I recall your smile, young
and carefree, a strong spirit,
like a lone wolf or bear cosy in his skin.
Scaling each rock with care,
you retrace the steps
of a legendary king
to arrive at the peak.

This is what I remember.

Below, summer grass waving
up at the rocky cliff face, where a fellow pilgrim
makes his slow descent.
Standing at the edge, your smile curls
into my chest, its curve breaking
beyond the frame   into the shocking white sky,
shattering any nocuous present.

Memory stone: In fragments

1   *Stones*

Stones can talk
but only to those who will listen.

To remember,
I collect a stone for each city.

2   *Dubrovnik*

Walking along ancient city walls,
we mark our descent
by strolling towards the jetty.

The waves come in, and rain starts to fall.
The ground gets wet, slippery
if not careful. You walk to the edge,

while I linger behind, curious
about a grey stone washed up
by the tide. Smooth, cold, it fits

into the curve of my palm.
This stone has seen rough days;
there are scars to prove it. See

how the sea has weathered
coarse edges round, twisting, scratching,
biting at hard rock. Her final gift,

a seaweed fossil pressed into
the stone's heart, a reminder of home,
before spitting it ashore.

3   *Pula*

Three hours in the Amphitheatre.
Before leaving, I slide three stones
into my pocket, light in my gloved hands.

White limestone fragments. My favourite
resembles a mountain range, with one sharp
and one flat peak. Jagged at the edges,

parts of it have turned grey from breathing
in the damp of the tropics.
The second stone is shorter, broader,

like a quiet resting toad. The smallest
reminds me of an onion bulb or a Hershey's Kiss.
Wobbly base, prickly tip.

Removed from their site of former glory,
these relics become ornamental.
I touch each imperfect piece—trace

the striated edges, indents in each rock,
and wake up again with the sun breaking
through white lace curtains,
Roman columns framed by the window.

4   *Motovun*

From this sleepy medieval walled town,
the stone I collect looks ordinary.

Grey, flat, shaped like an isosceles
trapezoid, parallel at two sides.

I turn it over, rubbing my thumb
and forefinger against its smooth face.

Like the place, this stone is a sleepy
checker piece, waiting for summer

and the film festival, where every empty space
turns into a camper's makeshift bed;

the dormant old town comes alive, swelling
with this heady influx.

But for now, it is December,
so we slow our walk to the hush

of the streets, pass by a church closed
for winter. We take our time

with a place we will not return to,
a town fortified in stone in time.

5   *Rovinj*

A crooked headland inches out to sea.
Of all the small ones, I love you best.
Smooth at the base, you are a rough-cut

wonder. Child of the Adriatic, fished
from her depths. In the old days,
fishermen's wives would gather

in the chapel to pray, only leaving
upon their husbands' safe return.
On the rocky shore, a white column keeps vigil

where the patron saint's sarcophagus
was reportedly found. Above the bell tower,
a weather vane's slow spin:

face to sea meant fair winds,
back to sea meant foul.

6   *Ensemble*

Now the stone from Dubrovnik sits
on my second-hand piano, beside a bundle
of sweetgrass. The smaller ones line
my living room console, sharing the weight
of their memories with dried pine cones from Dalat,
fallen leaves from a Japanese castle garden,
and bleached coral from the Mauritian coast.
Assorted objects that contain the history of home
away from home. Collected over time, they form
an ensemble of remembered places, a patchwork
of a traveller's sojourn through lands of eternal
spring, snowless winters, of drifting along the Adriatic
into the ocean's eye. Listen, undercurrents crash
beneath, waves breaking reef ashore.

Acknowledgements

Red Earth is firstly dedicated to my husband, Ethan Leong for his unwavering love and support, and with whom I journeyed to the many places that I write about in my poems. Secondly, *Red Earth*, particularly the poems about childhood, growing up and familial relationships are dedicated to my parents, Elaine Ke and Charles Vincent, for their love and encouragement. Despite not having completed their own formal education, they planted seeds of imagination, which imbued in me a passion and love for books and reading at an early age, enabling me to grow into the woman and writer that I am today. *Red Earth*, as its title suggests, is also written for the earth that is my home, dwelling place, and first mother, as well as all sentient beings that have taught me what it means to live with kindness, compassion and humility on earth as kin. Lastly, I would like to thank Boey Kim Cheng, my MA supervisor and mentor, for his patience, kindness, humility and wisdom, and to whom I owe the thanks for the title of this manuscript.

— The working manuscript, *Red Earth*, was a finalist in the Gaudy Boy Poetry Book Prize 2020 (New York)

The publication of individual poems is acknowledged below:

— "Flvctvat nec mergitvr" and "Inheritance" were first published in *Usawa Literary Review*

— "Pilgrims" and "Solar eclipse" were first published in *Portside Review*

— "Crossing" and "The Blue Mountains" were first published in *Atelier of Healing: Poetry About Trauma and Recovery* (Squircle Line Press)

— "Falcon" was first published in *Note for Note 2021: Universality Supreme* (The Arts House Singapore)

— "Family tree" and "Albatross" were first published in *Southeast Asian Review of English*

— "Throw me in the landfill" was first published in *Open Your Eyes: An anthology of climate change* (Hawakal Publishers)

— "The Blue Mountains" was shortlisted for Catharsis 2020 (Singapore Poetry Festival)

- "Inheritance" came in Second place for the National Poetry Competition 2020
- "Le Morne beach" was first published in @homeinsiberia, and later in *Portside Review*
- "Lost tongue" was first published in *Poetry Moves* (Ethos Books)
- "Sungei Buloh sonnets" and "Nondescript" were first published in *Quarterly Literary Review Singapore*
- An earlier version of "Red earth" was first published in *About Place Journal*
- "Island city" was first published in *Split Rock Review*, and later in *Contour: A Lyric Cartography of Singapore* (Pagesetters)
- "We have forgotten" was first published in *The Stinging Fly* and later in *Contour: A Lyric Cartography of Singapore* (Pagesetters)
- An earlier version of "Everything is perfect from far away" was first published in *Ghost City Review*
- An earlier version of "And at once I knew, I was not magnificent" was first published in *The Remembered Arts Journal*

About the Author

Esther Vincent Xueming is the editor-in-chief and founder of The Tiger Moth Review, an independent eco journal of art and literature based in Singapore. She is co-editor of two poetry anthologies, Poetry Moves (Ethos Books, 2020) and Little Things (Ethos Books, 2013), and Making Kin, an ecofeminist anthology of personal essays by women writers in Singapore (Ethos Books). The working manuscript of Red Earth was a finalist for the 2020 Gaudy Boy Poetry Book Prize (New York).

Red Earth
Esther Vincent

Copyright © 2021 Esther Vincent Xeuming

All rights reserved.

Cover & Interior Art: Chan Shu Yin
Cover Design & Layout: Zach Curtis

ISBN: 978-1-7368209-0-2

Second Edition

Blue Cactus Press | Tacoma, Washington

bluecactuspress.com

www.ingramcontent.com/pod-product-compliance
Lightning Source LLC
Chambersburg PA
CBHW042319090526
44583CB00025BA/3195